2109. DAYS OF LOVING YOU

SHAURYA CHAWLA

Made with ♥ on the Notion Press Platform
www.notionpress.com

Contents

1. Warm hugs of Poems.

2109 Days of loving you,
is about my love for her.
And how It felt differently on different days.

To the girl this is all about, you are not here, that's why my poems shout.
From the first time I saw you, the way you looked.
Your smile and heart, my breath it took.
Me talking about you is nothing new, But this time I wrote a *book for you.*

I loved the way you smiled.
Even more, I loved the way your smile made me smile
but I hate how much I drowned in your love when you left.

She was the poem, I was the verse
My love for her, my only curse
She was the mystery where I found me
Love in my dictionary originated from thee.

And with the night ends
I can calm the storms which yearned your love but never earned it.
Although if all of me wasn't enough for your sky
These storms are worth my cry.
And if I have ever been the one not enough
I'll never ask for you to showcase your bluff.
As if my love cannot fill your whole sky
It is not anymore worth my try.

The stars, fate, destiny,
If it doesn't lead to you, I don't wanna believe that it's true.
If not today, I wish to find you again,
Hopefully when love's magic rains.

From the start to the end
There was no finish line to begin
In the race of chasing my delusion of love with you,
reality won the race.

I hate it when you doubt your worth.
Ask me, you are the most precious thing on my little earth.
I know maybe you won't realize
Until you see yourself from my eyes.

I didn't fall in love with you just because your beauty grasps my breath, I fell in love with you because in 20 years I couldn't adore anyone the way I adore you. The beauty that your inner self holds is quite profound. There may be someone better, but I don't see that.
All I see and want is you.

I know I miss you,
Incomplete like a sunset without a view.
The harmony of you made my life a perfect song,
Without you in it, the melody feels so wrong.

What am I to you?

The question I asked is still unsolved. The mystery around this question is where my world revolves. If the answer is still the same, tell me why is it hard to say. I don't want the love, but my best friend I lost on the way.

The art of loving is formidable, not many people are artists.
It's easy to love the moon but not the darkness when it disappears.

I miss the way we used to be "us,"
Now it's just "you" and "me" which is not enough.
I know being the same way is tough,
Because the scars we left were too rough.

Leaving you hurted but staying any more Was piercing my heart daily until it drains out of your love.
So I chose to leave.

The urge to talk to you, how can I control?
The day starts with your thoughts and night ends with your soul.
I wonder how can someone overcome,
From the love of this kind,
when these petals of love are hard to find.

We were just Polaroids of imperfect pictures perfectly portrayed.

You were the poetry at its prime,
But the words of our poem didn't rhyme.
Though we synced sublime,
What went wrong? Was it the place or the wrong time?

I waited for you to say I mean something, that you need me, I needed you to say that you need me but you didn't and it broke my heart but still those broken pieces love you as *whole.*

I never knew how it feels to be loved,
But I always knew how it is to love.

You see that bittersweet irony.

I loved you in a way I yearned to be loved,
The simple boy filled with love,
Who gave it all away in hope to be left with just enough.
Though the love may not have been ideal,
It was untainted, and I gave it all,
Possibly till the time it fainted.

Love in stories is just a fiction not truth
The perfection is myth
All that love requires is efforts and bare minimum
And the heart syncs just when it hears something it never heard
The reality is scary, to find that love is unwary
The loads on the way is difficult to carry
But in the end who sticks to it, is the one, who fulfills our *myths and fairy.*

And now I know love won't *heal* the hearts of the ones it wasn't meant for.

I don't know how to love again,
It's been 6 years and I still feel the same.
The echoes of your voice now regain
Like fighting for love and losing that game.

From being a shot of espresso coffee that I stay awake
to being a sleeping pill that now I don't want to wake up.

My heart beats fast every time I see you
It's just a marathon I could never lose
It tries to be perfect in front of you
Because it is afraid to show its *imperfection*
As you might not choose it.

You filled the void in my heart such that now there is no space for anyone in it.

I hate it how she makes me feel, like she is the only one there
Her beauty so vivid that my eyes just stare
How will I let go if all my thoughts are still about you
The feelings untold and the words too.

When you look for the eyes that never saw you.
Love becomes *blind.*

It’s unhealthy how much I love you
The way I am aghast with the thought of life without you
I can learn not to love myself
But I will still look for you in the crowd, I am lost myself.

You lived in my heart which never belonged to me. As The *un-belongingness* of my heart belonged within you.

The,"I am okay" was just a lie
The truth, was crystal clear in your eye
The feelings unhidden, you tried to hide
I noticed in your silence how much you cried.

If someday you feel you don't matter just remember I wrote this book for you.
You will always matter to me.

In the quest of love I found something ineffable
When I had everything I couldn't keep it stable
When it's gone, Is when i realised the need
That it takes time to grow the plant from seed.

Praying for your well being above my own was a gesture of care hidden.
Even if it meant for my love to be forbidden.

For you I hope to wait,
but for me there is a barrier on your gate.
The question I ask is this my fate?
Or is this just a tempting bait,
For something good that awaits.

I know some stories are better unfinished but how can I explain it to the heart, when it's every beat connects to you, whenever it romanticise any fictional love story.

You don't deserve just moons and stars,
As they are ordinary beauty at par.
My love, even the moons and stars yearn to be like you.
You deserve someone to go that extra mile to make you believe it's true.

To love is to create, but to be loved is *fate*.

When you get lost, I'll find you
Because In some ways I knew you better then you did too.
Even in the cluster of stars I'll find mine
Because even in your darkness you'll still shine.

Unconditional love

Daily, I watered the flower in hope for you to receive those beautiful Lilies, but I never expected for you to keep it in your bouquet.

People say for me you are not right,
But my love for you will always win that fight.
I don't care what you might be in people's sight,
Because I was the one there listening to you every night.

"What's so special about her?" They ask

I don't think there needs to be anything special. It's all about accepting her the way she was, that's damn special. Loving the *misfits* of her rather than what fits.

You have a precious little heart
If it breaks, it will tear me apart
I want you to have all the happiness you deserve
And if it's any less I want you to have it from my reserve.

You said don't care for me, just like it meant nothing. It hurt. The first time in a long time, something truly hurt. I wanted to say let me care, let me be there, but I stayed quiet this time. That's when I promised myself never to come back until you asked me to. Just say the word, and I'll be there. No questions asked, I swear.

The journey of ours was like a fine wine
Even though the outcome wasn't aligned
I held onto it like it was just mine
But in the end our fate wasn't intertwined.

Against that mature face lies within a cute and notorious child.
The child in you made my heart smile.
More importantly, it brought the child in me out,
Which comes only with you and no one else, I doubt.

My face hides the truth that I am not doing well
After you left my life is a living hell
I wish you fought when I asked you to leave
Just told me I was wrong and wrong was my belief.

How beautiful is it when we love someone, we resonate with everything around us, though it doesn't make sense to others but ourselves.

I am not a heartbroken lover
Just an agent of love undercover
The pain I found and discover
Was nothing compared to the incomplete love I endeavor.

Even the moons look prettier to eyes from far
but when you look within it is filled with hollow holes which makes it beautiful.

You were that moon.

My heart bloomed with the fragrance of your soul.
The part missing in me, you made it whole.
Your daylight filled the blank space in my heart.
I always believed this love was evermore from the start.

On days when I don't feel like living for myself,

I live for you.

I may be shy but I will never shy out to express how I feel for you.
In front of everyone I'll choose you.
In days you don't choose yourself I'll choose you.
I'll love you in days I don't love myself
And I would never let you feel unloved and unworthy
because you are all the *worth* there is.

It's either the meaning of life with you in it or the purpose of life without you.

With you it's like everything or nothing at all, there is no in between.

Sit with me, talk about your day
I will just hear you say
Even the not so sensible talk is okay
I promise to make your heart smile and give shoulder to teary drops you lay.

I never believed home could be a person. I always thought it was just a metaphor to describe love. But then I met you, my *comfort peace*. It felt like I was as comfortable with you as I was with myself. That's when I realized how a person can be your home.

I wish you stayed a bit longer.
Our broken pieces could have been stronger.
That strong ache to hear your voice again.
Is like the dance of "Jab We Met" in the rain.

The time you choose others over me,
I still choose you.
That's how obtusely you mattered to me.

The night breeze isn't cold anymore.
The morning sun isn't bold anymore.
That innocent happiness is not like before,
As the keys are lost of your closed door.
How will I find the keys in those bundles?
Give me a passage so my heart doesn't fumble.

I moved across the ocean side, to see if there was a world where me and you collide. But I know there isn't, so the current situation is what I abide. In reality, all the manifestations and dreams died.

No one can take your place
Though the heart is hollow with void it creates
Many came and went but it only knows your face
Ah, that trenching love made me prisoner of this case.

You still are the most special one for me.
But maybe now I just live in your *memory*.

I made my peace with the fact that I won't have you anymore.
But how do I explain it to the heart when loving you is its core.
The fact that I ended the things is what I wish to ignore,
That by not wanting you, I just kept wanting you more.

I only believe in love because of the way I love you. That someone can love you unconditionally and keeps loving you no matter what. The day I stop loving you is the day I will stop believing there is love for me.

Time changes things but it won't change how I feel for you.
It is sometimes unexplainable but true.
I wish to age with you and grow old.
And I would still love you the same like I showed.

I was your *human diary,* you shared everything with me.
But now I am just lying in dust, hoping you would find me again to read it.

To be sure is unsure,
For this pain there is no cure.
To the joy which is just a decoy,
For the man inside this boy.
To be seen is unseen,
For the mystery I am keen.
To the many who became few,
All of it leads to *you*.

"How can I ignore when my Instagram feed is filled with all the surreal moments which I can't have with you."

She is the girl, for whom I can do the extra.
She is the girl, who is ordinarily extraordinary.
She is the girl, who I want to be my world.
She is the girl, who has priceless worth.
She is the girl, who sprinkles the light.
She is the girl, with whom everything feels just right.

The way you tripped I fell, like I was standing alone in the crowded hall. Still looking for you who wasn't even there, doing injustice to my heart which seemed fair.

I won't promise you forever which I don't know but I'll promise to treat you right,
Respect you,
Always listen to you,
never lash out my anger,
and most importantly
I promise to make you feel loved.

I wanted that bookish love with you. The one where all your dreams come true. You realise the meaning of love from the gestures I do. I treat you in a way that you never knew. The love that feels unreal, but in my reality it's the truth. How far-fetched was my dream that I wrote this book for you.

In the world of being a green forest or a red flag,
I will be your *silver lining* who doesn't need to be labelled to love you right.

I don't know how much depth there is that I still keep falling in love with you. There is no way out, is how deep I have fallen. Now there is emptiness that surrounds me with echoes of you.

I won't deny that I still love you.
The way my heart throbs, only at the beat of you.
The way my eyes are captured like there is no one else to be seen.
Why are you so magical is what I am keen.

I am very scared that I won't fall in love again.
I think my heart was only meant to love you. It just can't look at someone else the way it looks at you. I love how much my love is for you, but I am also scared of how much I love you.

How did we fall apart?
I think lack of communication was the art.
Isn't there a possibility to restart?
Because I would seize that with every beat of my heart.

I don't know whether I was what you need but, I cared, loved, ached for you more than I could ever conceal.

Just ask me once I'll stay.
I promise you I won't run away.
Let me hold your hand; I won't let it go.
I am not like others who do so.

When I see the night sky, all I see is you, my shining bright star. Even the moon withholds its beauty against you.

The way you moved on, it chafes.
But I am happy, as happiness for you is all I crave.
Though I act all strong and brave,
But against my love for you I am just a slave.

I tried. It wasn't easy to let you go; my heart throbbed with the thought of you leaving. But if I wouldn't have taken that step, I guess we wouldn't even have so little of what we have now.

Portrait of my life pictured you,
The elegance of it was unimaginably true.
Now something is missing and I guess it's you.
Just hold my hand and paint it through.
The picture will be complete just like new.

I felt alive with you. Like there was something to live for. Even the memories of you make me vulnerable.
That hidden cuteness in teasing each other, to irritating each other till we lose our minds. I came a long way. But more importantly I still hold you. I just don't know why, I guess there is no possible explanation of how I feel for you.

I was never the one cared,
But always the one prepared
To spread the love, to care, to take your pain,
Even when the darkness was running through my veins.

The heart stabbed with your thoughts bleeds with your love.
How will it survive? How will it be ever enough?
Heal the wounds, you are its aid,
the bleeding would stop and the pain would fade.

How does my smile glow,
With a single message of your hello.
How can I control myself, how can I let go,
When yours is the only message where my smile shows.

I hope you'll remember me in days which aren't fair, that there was someone always to take care. Who never asked for love, just wanted to give and you treated him like ordinary and made him leave.

Now calling your name feels strange.
Yesterday you were my monkey and today it's all changed.
I think I needed this pain to be where I am,
Else I would have been forever stuck in your traffic jam.

I choose the path for myself, where the pain beholds me. I live with it everyday, loving you whilst not having you in my life. Just as thorns might hurt holding onto a beautiful flower.

I will put up with your tantrum.
They are not a burden to me.
I will never make you feel like a problem.
As your words are the music that I see.

When I read our old texts, my eyes are numb. How did that beautiful bond end? Why were we so dumb?
Bonds like that are rare to be found.
The frolic talks and the care in rebound.

The caretaker I became, I took the care.
In your happiness and sorrow, I took the share.
I never left you alone, I couldn't dare.
But what about me, were you ever there?

Promises were made but we both didn't keep.
Those words weren't lies but these wounds are *deep*.

How peaceful are your thoughts?
It fulfills that emptiness drought.
The intensity of it, staying in my mind,
Is just like you, one of a kind.

Saw your post today how wholesome you looked. Just looking at your picture my eyes were overwhelmed with emotions. I can't stop falling in love with you, how can I not love you? You are everything I could ever ask for. You are beautiful like rain, who washes away every droplet of pain.

I shivered when you left,
my hands were numb.
The eyes were watery,
and the dreams were dumb.
This is when I realised
a sense of loss.

I never had any doubts when it came to you. There were no ifs and buts.
You were My Chicago.

We are all doomed when in love.
The silence starts to murmur and the words aren't enough.
Why are we so startled? When things are tough?
As there is no justice to be done above.

I knew the day wasn't far, where the morning won't start with your text. Even the sunrise was from the west. My life wasn't the same after that. I was doomed in the flame and my love burned even through ashes. I am still walking on the hellfire in hope to reach you, though with burned scars, which only your love can heal. Even if in the end you don't choose me, I would love to be burned watching you.

Everyone has multiple faces,
Which comes out in different times and phases.
Whatever good and bad of mine came out was real,
Not tried to show anyone, only you knew the deal.

I know you won't love me, but I'll still love you. My love wasn't bounded with the expectation to have it back.
I'll always love you.

My love is not mad,
The part of it is just too scared.
For the hope to have this kind of love again,
The possibility I think is negligible to insane.

The message unsent

It's been a while since we had an honest conversation. I am worried about how you are doing.

I know I am not there anymore to be there for you. I miss being there for you, taking care of you, not allowing your precious heart to break. Even though sometimes I maybe was the cause it suffered the pain, and I am sorry that I am not there to take that pain away.

Some days are very difficult without you. Everything is going okay but it suddenly hits the thoughts of you, you not being here. How much I miss you that I cannot tell, and the worst part is I cannot tell you. So I empty these thoughts by crying in hope to rise stronger tomorrow.

For the first time when I choose myself over you.
You left.
That's the price of self love.

It was not about doing the right thing for you,
as in love all the wrongs seem more right.

I got tired of love.
But I never got tired of loving if it meant loving you.

With the blink of an eye, things changed.
Last night I was talking with you like I don't know how to sleep.
In the morning, it feels like a dream, like you were never there in my reality.

I hope I did right by you.
That there weren't times where the air you breathed was polluted by me.

You are different. I don't know if it's my love that makes you different or you actually are the One of the many. But it's different with you than with anyone else. I am different with you than I am with anyone else.

The origami of childhood love,
Is still the art, which is my favorite.
The innocence of this love is the best trait.
From nothing to the best we create
To Something that is worth our wait.

It was the first time when so little of someone meant so much to me.
When my eyes saw your shadow, it framed your picture to see.

Even in your drought, I waited for the rain.
Instead of going to the ocean to get rid of pain.

And when you feel unloved,
just remember,
Even the scars are beautiful when looked from the eyes of its surgeon.
It always depends on that person.
I hope you know you are loved by me.

Love is what makes you, love is what breaks you.
Love is what changes you, love is what makes you,
you.

When I can't sleep I think about you,
Because in these late nights I had you.
Now I sleep early to avoid your thoughts,
Else the night will be full of memories my heart fought.

If my love was never meant to be yours
Then why did it fill me with empty decors?
Now I still believe in love though with an empty heart
In that broken piece you are the missing part.

I am still stuck in the time.
Where you and I used to meet after school gets over because we were too shy to talk in front of everyone and those few minutes of talking with you felt like,

no one has ever held me like you did.

.

It's been 6 years of my diploma in love and I still haven't graduated.

Being away from you, I realised the comfort I lost with you.
I found peace in your thoughts.

When my heart was a forest filled with trees you made your home there,
Just to cut down the trees which were not yours to share.
Now the empty forest is what I bare,
And how can I hate you when I know you won't care.

And when you wake up without a smile on your face just remember,
You are like a canvas painted with just the perfect colors which are *rarely* found.

If love was meant to be so beautiful
Then why do these curtains drape the sunlight in my darkness?
When all I ever did was *shine* the darkened places.

For the feeling of love you were the perfect epitome.
When I was lost, in you I found my home.
Now my eyes are filled with tears, not because of sorrow
But because I am filled with love, that I didn't borrow.

If I was ever asked about love my tale will always tell your story.
Knowing the love wasn't mine I still fought for the glory.
My story wasn't supposed to have a happy ending,
As it was not a love story just one sided love pretending.

How do I feel about you?
There aren't enough words I can form to tell you the truth but I'll give it a try.
With every knot of thread I tie it creates your design.
Even with the imperfect design I only want this to be called mine.
When there is only one moon why would I even search for any other,
As even with its disappearance or different shape I would still see it as whole.

I can see no other girl, my eyes just crave your sight
Speaking about you, writing about you and thinking
about you is such a delight.
Just talking with you used to make my day
Now without you I am just trying to be okay.

In the generation where the relationship changes in a day,
My love for you will always stay.

I would always be grateful to you. You made that innocent child into a loving and caring man, who feels happy to spread love and care, even if sometimes he has to *sacrifice* his own.

I always wondered was there ever a moment where your heart wanted mine? Maybe even for a fleeting second.

I hope you know
I'll be there, when you will have no one to care.
I'll be there, when weights in your heart are difficult to share
I'll be there, when your eyes are filled with tears
I'll be there, when being vulnerable is your fear
I'll be there, when being in love feels scary.
I'll be there, because I'll always care.

If truth is what makes you stay
I'll tell the lies of I am okay
Because as much as I want you I know you don't
As your words may tell the truth but your actions won't.

I have nothing but words for you which I never knew could be formed to describe someone who is a whole *dictionary*.

By trying to be everything for you I was left with nothing for myself.

The hearts that look light are heavy inside filled with love, which never reached.

And, When you leave the greenery of gardens you find emptiness of sand in the desert.
That's how love feels like *without you.*

The journey ends here this is the last stop
The best one by far, mic drop.
These words won't suffice my love, they cannot.
But still I hope you remember me, not just a memory you forgot.
This is not for a closure, I understood that a long time ago.
That a love which isn't reciprocated is the love to let go.

www.ingramcontent.com/pod-product-compliance
Lightning Source LLC
LaVergne TN
LVHW021155160826
845679LV00024B/2133

* 9 7 9 8 8 9 4 4 6 4 2 2 0 *